LOVE
God's Greatest Gift

John Mark Pool

LOVE
God's Greatest Gift

Lion and Lamb art by Robert Bartow   www.bartowimages.com

Published by Word to the World Ministries and Keep Safe, Inc.
P.O. Box 879 • Baker, LA 70704-0879
225.771.1774
www.wordtotheworldministries.org

Dedication

I dedicate this book to the love of my life, my compassionate wife, Sandy Pool. She is my best friend, God-given and ordained ministry partner, wonderful helpmate and a great encourager in everything the Lord has called me to do. Throughout my life, my anointed mother Loriece Pool will forever be an abiding and loving spiritual inspiration. This book is also dedicated to my very talented and beautiful daughters Raegan and Allison Pool; I love you both so much and pray you will always continue to be messengers of God's unconditional love. Most of all, this book is dedicated to the Lord Jesus Christ who is the everlasting giver of unconditional love.

"And now abide faith, hope, love, these three; but the greatest of these is love." 1 Corinthians 13:13

"For God so loved the world that He gave His only begotten Son, that whoever believes in Him should not perish but have everlasting life." John 3:16

Acknowledgments

I wish to thank my anointed spiritual moms: Mom O'deal Jefferson, Nora "Nonnie" Hitte Hammonds, Mama Lillie Mauldin, Dr. Mary Ruth Swope and so many precious others that have adopted me. I know you pray fervently and constantly for me, as I continue to feel your unconditional love and blessings. I have sincere and heartfelt appreciation for my wonderful mother- and father-in-law, Russell and Dorothy Montgomery, since you both are such a blessing and a very special part of my life. Susan Goebel, thank you for sowing into the ministry with faith, love and countless hours of diligent work. Pastors Lynn and Betty Hildreth, because of the encouragement you have given me to continue in the calling of God during some of my life's most difficult trials, you will always have my heart's depth of gratitude. This wholehearted gratefulness also goes out to Don and Joel Nori who are instruments in God's hand to help me fulfill my God-given destiny and God's burgeoning dream for my life. I am also tremendously appreciative for all the encouragement, prayers, and blessings of my friend, Steve Jones, and the many people, ministries, and churches that have contributed so much to help us take God's powerful Word to the World. May the Lord bless you! — *John Mark Pool*

"And now abide faith, hope, love, these three; but the greatest of these is love." 1 Corinthians 13:13

"For God so loved the world that He gave His only begotten Son, that whoever believes in Him should not perish but have everlasting life." John 3:16

TABLE OF CONTENTS

"And now abide faith, hope, love, these three; but the greatest of these is love." 1 Corinthians 13:13

"For God so loved the world that He gave His only begotten Son, that whoever believes in Him should not perish but have everlasting life." John 3:16

"And now abide faith, hope, love, these three;
but the greatest of these is love." 1 Corinthians 13:13

"For God so loved the world that He gave His only
begotten Son, that whoever believes in Him should
not perish but have everlasting life." John 3:16

Introduction

It is the purpose and will of God for every one of us to receive and share His unconditional love with others. Without love we are nothing but a noisy gong. All that matters is determined by the love present. Not just any love will do; it must be pure and given by God to stand the test of time and all the arrows thrown by the devil. This unconditional love of God is the glue that binds the brokenhearted and heals the wounds of life's many battles. Let us discover that after all the efforts and words fail, we must simply give unconditional love an opportunity to grow and show its power to transform. Love is the answer God has already prepared to serve to His hungry creation. Love never fails, but instead prevails and conquers all. Let Love fill us up and completely satisfy us in knowing and loving our Lord and Savior Jesus Christ by a demonstration to others of the unconditional love that our merciful God has shown us.   *— John Mark Pool*

"And now abide faith, hope, love, these three; but the greatest of these is love." 1 Corinthians 13:13

"For God so loved the world that He gave His only begotten Son, that whoever believes in Him should not perish but have everlasting life." John 3:16

Chapter 1

God's Greatest Gift

It is such a familiar scripture reading. Many people who have been raised in any evangelical Christian church have been introduced to 1st Corinthians chapter 13, or the Love Chapter of the New Testament.

"And now abide faith, hope, love, these three; but the greatest of these is love" (1 Corinthians 13:13).

However, something has happened to the practice of this one gift that God identifies as the greatest of all His gifts.

Perhaps you are immediately thinking, "Here comes the 'knock out punch' sermon covered with the love commandment." This is the type of unnecessary rebuke a preacher may give because you did not go help the destitute this week at the shelter on the other side of town. When we listen to this type of preaching, we often feel guilty and ashamed.

We need to stop distressing about our repressed feelings of guilt that satan injects totally from our religious-based conscience. We must cheer up and not be oppressed by such feelings. These thoughts of guilt and unworthiness are brought upon us by satan. Your child's choir concert or baseball game, recital, mother's or father's birthdays and many other family events are the most important things in the world. They certainly are in my life. Family should be foremost in all our lives. Ministry is love of our family—God's main church model. For Jesus Christ, His physical family was somewhat integrated with His ministry family, as they had fellowship often. Jesus gave us this example in the first Shabbat model, the Lord's Supper, as He demonstrated the importance of fellowship with family, breaking bread and giving thanks to God not only on the Sabbath but each and every day. We should emulate this lifestyle daily, since Jesus gave it to us to follow.

This subject goes much deeper than missing choir practice before a major church presentation. It demands far more attention than decorating the sanctuary until midnight for the mission convention. This is about a way of life that will revolutionize your spiritual walk as a believer in Jesus Christ.

Just travel with me for a while down this road to contemplate some thoughts we may have about others we have known. Do you remember ever meeting a stranger who did not talk much, did not attract much attention in a crowd, but to whom you seemed drawn nonetheless? I certainly have. People like this just seem so at ease, listening to our every word and smiling genuinely at the points we make. We may see him or her quietly slipping out discreetly to pick up a dropped notebook or collect the coffee cups around the table while others keep visiting and going on with rapid-fire conversation. No task is either too great or too menial for him to accomplish if it means putting a smile on someone's face. We have probably noticed this person's disposition is a way of life.

He is the one we turn to for that quiet personal conversation, because we have unconditional acceptance and love in his presence. A glow of unconditional love radiates from the countenance of this compassionate person. We continue to enjoy the feeling of total acceptance whenever we are near. It inspires us to radiate the love of Jesus from deep within our spirits. Matthew 5:16 says, ***"Let your light so shine before men, that they may see your good works and glorify your Father in heaven."*** The qualities we want to model the most are unconditional love, acceptance and forgiveness, just as Jesus modeled these for us by his infusion of love into His intimate ministry family—His twelve disciples.

I, too, want to be "accepted in the beloved" in the type of intimate ministry family that Jesus displayed. ***"to the praise of the glory of His grace, by which He made us accepted in the***

Beloved" (Ephesians 1:6). He totally devoted His personal ministry of love on earth in the world's first church model. Jesus Christ taught by mentoring His close-knit family of twelve disciples. He knew they would make many mistakes, that they would vacillate and question Him. Nevertheless, Jesus continued to be "love in life" to them. Not one of them had ever before experienced this truly loving example Jesus was portraying. They did not understand this type of "love in life" at first, yet later, all but a couple of the disciples died for it.

That sounds like someone you have heard a lot about throughout your lives. You know whom I am talking about now, and you are right. It is Almighty God in the form of Love for His creation lived out in the redemptive Human-God Form called "Yeshua, our Messiah." Jesus Christ of Nazareth is the only Messiah and Savior of the world. He gave us His unconditional love by His total obedience to Almighty God's plan—even to the death on a cross. Jesus said it himself, ***"This is My commandment, that you love one another as I have loved you. Greater love has no one than this, than to lay down one's life for his friends" (John 15:12-13).***

One day as I was living the nominal church-going, middle American, "Christendom lifestyle" that included compromise for a few self-indulgences, the Lord spoke to me through His Word. During one of my fits of desperation, I grabbed my carry-to-church-on-Sunday Bible. Then He took me to John 14:15 that says, ***"If you love me, keep my commandments."*** I had certainly read that verse before, but today it soaked deep into my spirit as if I had read this scripture for the first time. I said, "Lord, I know I am not keeping your commandments all the time, and I have lots of areas I have not turned over to you." All this began to flood my spirit. Understanding swept over me as I recalled what my dad always said, "Son, remember, actions speak louder than words."

Now my heavenly Father was saying the same thing to my spirit-man about my actions. They spoke loudly and clearly. Then the Lord said, "You say you love Me, but you really love yourself and your selfish lifestyle more than Me." I felt such sorrow at that moment that I had been so selfish and lived such a lie. For the first time in my life I had to come to grips with the fact that I was on the throne trying to convince all those around me that I loved the Lord. Then, after nearly drowning in tears of repentance, I started loving God more than ever before.

"Have mercy upon me, O God, according to Your lovingkindness; according to the multitude of Your tender mercies, blot out my transgressions. Wash me thoroughly from my iniquity, and cleanse me from my sin. For I acknowledge my transgressions, and my sin is always before me. Against You, You only, have I sinned, and done this evil in Your sight— That You may be found just when You speak, and blameless when You judge.

"Behold, I was brought forth in iniquity, and in sin my mother conceived me. Behold, You desire truth in the inward parts, and in the hidden part You will make me to know wisdom. Purge me with hyssop, and I shall be clean; wash me, and I shall be whiter than snow. Make me hear joy and gladness, that the bones You have broken may rejoice. Hide Your face from my sins, and blot out all my iniquities.

"Create in me a clean heart, O God, and renew a steadfast spirit within me. Do not cast me away from Your presence, and do not take Your Holy Spirit from me. Restore to me the joy of Your salvation, and uphold me by Your generous Spirit. Then I will teach transgressors Your ways, and sinners shall be converted to You. Deliver me from the guilt of bloodshed, O God, the God of my salvation, and my tongue shall sing aloud of Your righteousness.

"O Lord, open my lips, and my mouth shall show forth Your praise. For You do not desire sacrifice, or else I would give it; You do not delight in burnt offering. The sacrifices of God are a broken spirit, a broken and a contrite heart—these, O God, You will not despise" *(Psalms 51:1-17).*

After the Lord's resurrection in John 21:15b, Jesus asked Peter while serving him earthly food, *"...Do you love Me more than these?"* He posed this question to His disciples, and the question still remains for all of us today. Remember, you cannot know this answer without accepting Yeshua, Jesus Christ, as your Messiah. *"So when they had eaten breakfast, Jesus said to Simon Peter, 'Simon, son of Jonah, do you love Me more than these?' He said to Him, 'Yes, Lord; You know that I love You.' He said to him, 'Feed My lambs'" (John 21:15).*

It must be clearly understood, though, that you must love the Lord Jehovah, Elohim, before you can love others. Do you remember when the young lawyer confronted Jesus with the question about which commandment is the greatest?

"And when the multitudes heard this, they were astonished at His teaching.

"But when the Pharisees heard that He had silenced the Sadducees, they gathered together. Then one of them, a lawyer, asked Him a question, testing Him, and saying, 'Teacher, which is the great commandment in the law?'

"Jesus said to him, 'YOU SHALL LOVE THE LORD YOUR GOD WITH ALL YOUR HEART, WITH ALL YOUR SOUL, AND WITH ALL YOUR MIND.' This is the first and great commandment. And the second is like it: 'YOU SHALL LOVE YOUR NEIGHBOR AS YOURSELF.' On these two commandments hang all the Law and the Prophets" (Matthew 22:33-40). *Emphasis Added*

"And now abide faith, hope, love, these three; but the greatest of these is love." 1 Corinthians 13:13

"For God so loved the world that He gave His only begotten Son, that whoever believes in Him should not perish but have everlasting life." John 3:16

"And now abide faith, hope, love, these three;
but the greatest of these is love." 1 Corinthians 13:13

"For God so loved the world that He gave His only
begotten Son, that whoever believes in Him should
not perish but have everlasting life." John 3:16

Chapter 2

First Love God; Only Then Can We Love Others

It is only after we have accepted Jesus Christ as our personal Lord and Savior that we can accomplish the above. No matter what anyone has taught us, the Word of God is very clear that we cannot "Love our neighbor as ourselves" without Christ as our Savior, for if we do not have Jesus as our Savior, then we do not know God. If we do not really know God, then we cannot know ourselves. How can we love others as ourselves if we do not even know ourselves? Each and every one of us must make a decision in our "will-mind" that God created in us. Jesus loved us unconditionally and displayed this in His interactions with His twelve disciples. Christ was not in a pulpit hammering home a three-point sermon on a lifestyle of obedience to God. He was on the shore where they lived, preparing, calling and serving them a "feast of love" that compelled them to take the total baptismal plunge of His eternally transforming "love-immersion."

However, at the very moment when I was reading John 14:15 that says, **"If you love Me, keep My commandments,"** the one real God on the real throne spoke to me and said, *"I will not share My glory with anyone!"* This reality began to sink deep within my spirit, and I admitted to God right then that I did not really love Him as my Lord. Was I a Christian or was I living entirely for the devil? Had I really believed in my heart that I did not love the Lord even after having made a public confession of my salvation? All of these questions began rolling through my head. I certainly wanted to believe I was okay with the Lord. I had been convinced by many a preacher that as long as I attended church, went through the motions, said the right things and checked off the items on the Christian performance checklist, I was just fine in "the Christendom camp." However, I was not fine in my inner man; I was spiritually sick. I was lost, but looking for answers. I wanted to fit Christianity into my lifestyle. I wanted to be the ultimate boss of all decisions and rationalizations, so I just smeared the right lingo over the choices I made to better preserve my secret freedoms. These in essence had become the kingdoms of my heart. I was unwilling to allow those "sacred grounds" to be captured by any preacher, ministry, church, denomination or religion. I had played into the humanistic theology that approached God "my way." In my selfish flesh, God never recognized me. They were my kingdoms, and He said very clearly to me in I Corinthians 15:50b, ***"...flesh and blood cannot inherit the kingdom of God; nor does corruption inherit incorruption."***

I was the epitome of compromise. I selected churches that accommodated my lifestyle because I said, "After all, everything is done in moderation." I liked my social cocktails with people after work. I enjoyed the community fathers around me in my business environment and then around me again on Sunday mornings for noticeable nods to God at the "First Church of the Compromised Christian." What a lifestyle I had learned to "lie," I mean, "live."

You know the lifestyle. It is a life of checks and balances: Did I appear successful to the outside world in all of the crucial areas on my checklist of civic virtues?

- Career
- Status
- Family
- Success
- Community
- Church

Just as in my own case, it seemed as long as we, the good people of the community, could make checks by most of the "checks and balance blocks," we were on the right road toward "The Great American Dream."

When career consultants interviewed me about the above blocked categories during an advancement or career path change, I was always proud to cover all the bases by checking church membership.

We might have even felt better if our business associates of the same "First Nominal Church" sat on the same boards for the United Fund Drives and golfed with us on Saturday mornings followed by Bloody Marys at the 19th Hole Lounge. Since satan had deceived me, I thought that I was living right, life was good and I was just fine. So how did an end ever come to the selfish "kingdoms-of-my-heart" type of lifestyle? Just one special heart to heart talk with God when my dad was dying completely convinced me to repent and let God really change my life. (For more details, please read *Path of a Prophet*)

I am not degrading our American freedoms that are based on rewards for living right. I am very thankful for the truly wonderful people serving our country who sacrifice so much to support our lifestyle of cherished democracy. This includes many honest, law-abiding citizens with a heart to be part of a great moral society, whether they are Christian or not. That is not what I mean when I discuss the spiritual aspects of approaching God based on man's goodness. Many fine, upstanding moral citizens actually enjoy assisting the Christian community, yet may not ever make a personal commitment for Jesus Christ as their Lord.

Often people seek fulfillment of inner peace in the wrong places. It is tragic that so many people even live to defend their form of Christianity based merely on their righteousness and in their own strength. When they face difficult times, their ideals are shattered and many "cave in" because they have not learned to rest in God's grace during the various crises of life. These crises may include divorce, death of a loved one, severe health issues or any other tragic loss. We each have the courage, with God's grace, to face anything without "caving in!" **"*...My grace is sufficient for you, for My strength is made perfect in weakness..." (2 Corinthians 12:9).***

Drugs, smoking, alcohol, over-eating, gossiping, over-spending, pornography, gambling, and many other sins insulate scores of people from the emptiness that accompanies the pretense they live, but this never satisfies their spirit-man. Still others seek extramarital affairs to compensate for the love they cannot feel, because the Lord is locked out of their hearts. God's unconditional love will completely fill this void and the need for a pleasing and loving relationship. When we understand the gratifying and real true love of the Lord, we will not need to seek any other substitute. We find the love of the father so secure that we will never want anything to disrupt our having a satisfying relationship with our loving Father. We allow this love to completely restore us from a life of compromise to a totally un-compromised love with our Lord Jesus Christ.

Life's crises are often the catalysts for change in the lifestyle of the compromised person. Why? It is quite simple and can be defined in one word: self-surrender. Crises lead many people to "come to the end of themselves" and surrender completely to God's will. Since there is no fulfillment from the flesh, and because it breeds only shallowness, there is finally recognition that nothing is gained in the spirit man by trusting in the flesh.

"Let not mercy and truth forsake you; bind them around your neck, write them on the tablet of your heart, and so find favor and high esteem in the sight of God and man. Trust in the LORD with all your heart, and lean not on your own understanding; in all your ways acknowledge Him, and He shall direct your paths. Do not be wise in your own eyes; fear the LORD and depart from evil. It will be health to your flesh, and strength to your bones" (Proverbs 3:3-8).

"And now abide faith, hope, love, these three;
but the greatest of these is love." 1 Corinthians 13:13

"For God so loved the world that He gave His only
begotten Son, that whoever believes in Him should
not perish but have everlasting life." John 3:16

"And now abide faith, hope, love, these three; but the greatest of these is love." 1 Corinthians 13:13

"For God so loved the world that He gave His only begotten Son, that whoever believes in Him should not perish but have everlasting life." John 3:16

Chapter 3

Selfishness — Plain and Simple

We want it our way. We like it our way. We are taught from birth to be a strong person, to go out there and win the world. We may hear, "Conquer the business kingdom. Do not come home without that top-level executive career. Whatever it takes, just do it." That is why there are so many disappointed people today. We strictly equate money with success. Money has replaced virtue and character. The acquisition of money, money and more money rules our lifestyle and pursuits of happiness.

Once we get it our way, we have nothing to turn to during life's crises. Why is the dream so disappointing when we finally arrive? On the other hand, do we ever feel as if we have arrived? If we feel that we have, then we really must keep talking ourselves into it daily, for it is so shallow, entirely empty and utterly unfulfilling. If our kingdom is built simply on shifting sand, we can be sure life will continually lack peace and be extremely rough and unsettled. We might even be tempted to say, "I'm coming unglued," or "I just can't keep it together."

You may wonder if those who reach a pinnacle of success in the business world and accumulate a large financial net worth are "the bad people." I certainly hope not. Money is not evil; rather, it is the love of money that creates problems in our spiritual lives. If a person's basis for the pursuit of success is grounded on the love of money, he will never be spiritually satisfied.

"For the love of money is a root of all kinds of evil, for which some have strayed from the faith in their greediness, and pierced themselves through with many sorrows" (1 Timothy 6:10).

Our motives matter to God since He knows the very intentions of our hearts. *"The LORD doesn't make decisions the way you do! People judge by outward appearance, but the LORD looks at a person's thoughts and intentions." (1 Samuel 16:7b NLT).*

Let us consider an example. Although at times I was not always consistent in my preparation and path to this goal, I have wanted to speak and write books since I was a child. Would I now like to write a book that is a best seller? Of course I would. That also would be an added bonus because I would be most elated if the populace had chosen for a moment in time to read an inspired word that would better their lives. Would I be pleased with the monetary gain that accompanied the sales of my book as it makes the bestseller list? Why, certainly. Are the previously mentioned goals my inspiration as I sit at my keyboard? No. I think of sharing the inspiration, revelation and encouragement of the Word of God with the many hurting people in the world.

Writers who have the above-mentioned list of goals are not necessarily wrong for wanting these things, but I believe a truly professional writer works on issues and fundamental inspirations, knowing some days the writing will be easy, moving with fluid inspiration, but most days it will be plain old work. On these days it will take perseverance as the driving force to accomplish the goal successfully.

As a young journalist, I fancied myself as one who would uncover deep investigative secrets and unveil truths that could merit attention for my writing. Instead, I uncovered an election fraud in my local community and was scorched at city hall to the point of losing all my information sources. You see, motives are everything in our pursuit of being honest before God. Do I write for money? I hope the money accompanies the work, but that is not my motivating force. Instead, I hope to make money from my writings and use it as a valuable tool in serving Almighty God. For me, success is now building the Kingdom of God in any area God chooses to use me to work and serve Him.

God expects us to use the talents He gives us, but He does not usually start us out with five. Remember the parable of the talents? He gave different people different amounts. Many of us want to start out at five, but are given only one. Did we bury our one talent, or did we double it in an effort to build the Kingdom of God for our Heavenly Master? The best test for us to use as Christians is to see if we are cooperating with God's mandate to bring His Kingdom to "earth as it is in Heaven." We should always ask ourselves, "For whom am I really doing this? Am I doing it for the glory of God or for my personal gain?" We also need to ask ourselves, "Why am I doing this?" If we can honestly answer these questions correctly before God, then we will have no problem with our successes as Christians.

"For the kingdom of heaven is like a man traveling to a far country, who called his own

servants and delivered his goods to them. And to one he gave five talents, to another two, and to another one, to each according to his own ability; and immediately he went on a journey. Then he who had received the five talents went and traded with them, and made another five talents. And likewise he who had received two gained two more also. But he who had received one went and dug in the ground, and hid his lord's money.

"After a long time the lord of those servants came and settled accounts with them. So he who had received five talents came and brought five other talents, saying, 'Lord, you delivered to me five talents; look, I have gained five more talents besides them.' His lord said to him, 'Well done, good and faithful servant; you were faithful over a few things, I will make you ruler

over many things. Enter into the joy of your lord.'

"He also who had received two talents came and said, 'Lord, you delivered to me two talents; look, I have gained two more talents besides them.' His lord said to him, 'Well done, good and faithful servant; you have been faithful over a few things, I will make you ruler over many things. Enter into the joy of your lord.'

"Then he who had received the one talent came and said, 'Lord, I knew you to be a hard man, reaping where you have not sown, and gathering where you have not scattered seed. And I was afraid, and went and hid your talent in the ground. Look, there you have what is yours.' But his lord answered and said to him, 'You wicked and lazy servant, you knew that I reap where I have not sown, and gather where I

have not scattered seed. So you ought to have deposited my money with the bankers, and at my coming I would have received back my own with interest. So take the talent from him, and give it to him who has ten talents. For to everyone who has, more will be given, and he will have abundance; but from him who does not have, even what he has will be taken away. And cast the unprofitable servant into the outer darkness. There will be weeping and gnashing of teeth.'

"When the Son of Man comes in His glory, and all the holy angels with Him, then He will sit on the throne of His glory. All the nations will be gathered before Him, and He will separate them one from another, as a shepherd divides his sheep from the goats. And He will set the sheep on His right hand, but the goats on the left. Then the King will say to those on His right hand, 'Come, you blessed of My Father, inherit

the kingdom prepared for you from the foundation of the world'" (Matthew 25:14-34).

"And now abide faith, hope, love, these three; but the greatest of these is love." 1 Corinthians 13:13

"For God so loved the world that He gave His only begotten Son, that whoever believes in Him should not perish but have everlasting life." John 3:16

"And now abide faith, hope, love, these three; but the greatest of these is love." 1 Corinthians 13:13

"For God so loved the world that He gave His only begotten Son, that whoever believes in Him should not perish but have everlasting life." John 3:16

Chapter 4

Love in Action— No Matter What

People often attempt to build on shifting sand rather than the solid foundation of trust in Jesus' Word. During the period of "shifting sand" is exactly the prescribed perfect timing for God's unconditional love to be displayed. Simply prepare and serve that "meal of unconditional love" to the crisis victim facing the disaster and anyone else who gets "knocked off their feet" or thrown off track. Many of life's blows are designed by the prince of darkness and hit us without warning. Only by the Lord's timely display of redemptive love in action can people who are hurting be rescued from satan's grip. Are the life blows of these people their own fault? Does it matter? Since when did Jesus use blame or fault as the basis for us to decide to obey His command to love unconditionally? Did you see Jesus walk up and ask the sinners who was at fault for their sins? Jesus knew He would actually break the shame barrier in our lives for good. Of course we are at fault; we are flesh and blood living in a sinful world. That is the essence of the Lord's message of salvation.

"Is it not to share your bread with the hungry, and that you bring to your house the poor who are cast out; when you see the naked, that you cover him, and not hide yourself from your own flesh? Then your light shall break forth like the morning, your healing shall spring forth

speedily, and your righteousness shall go before you; the glory of the LORD shall be your rear guard. Then you shall call, and the LORD will answer; you shall cry, and He will say, 'Here I am.'

"If you take away the yoke from your midst, the pointing of the finger, and speaking wickedness, if you extend your soul to the hungry and satisfy the afflicted soul, then your light shall dawn in the darkness, and your darkness shall be as the noonday. The LORD will guide you continually, and satisfy your soul in drought, and strengthen your bones; you shall be like a watered garden, and like a spring of water, whose waters do not fail. Those from among you shall build the old waste places; you shall raise up the foundations of many generations; and you shall be called the Repairer of the Breach, The Restorer of Streets to Dwell In" (Isaiah 58:7-12).

"And now abide faith, hope, love, these three; but the greatest of these is love." 1 Corinthians 13:13

"For God so loved the world that He gave His only begotten Son, that whoever believes in Him should not perish but have everlasting life." John 3:16

Chapter 5

Messengers of Love?

Have you ever had someone come visit you during a crisis and begin to extol all the virtues of living a godly and holy life compared to the mess you had brought upon yourself? Do you remember fondly the teacher that loved you in spite of your mistakes rather than the one that placed you in front of the class and made a public spectacle of your misfortune? Which do you prefer? Do you personally want to invite over Job's wife and friends that tongue-lashed him continually with condemnation? *"Then his wife said to him, 'Do you still hold fast to your integrity? Curse God and die!' But he said to her, 'You speak as one of the foolish women speaks. Shall we indeed accept good from God, and shall we not accept adversity?' In all this Job did not sin with his lips. Now when Job's three friends heard of all this adversity that had come upon him, each one came from his own place…" (Job 2:9-11a).*

Or would you prefer to have the living example of our Savior, Jesus Christ, as He said, *"…I thank You, Father, Lord of heaven and earth, that You have hidden these things from the wise and prudent and have revealed them to babes. Even so, Father, for so it seemed good in Your sight. All things have been delivered to Me by*

My Father, and no one knows the Son except the Father. Nor does anyone know the Father except the Son, and the one to whom the Son wills to reveal Him. Come to Me, all you who labor and are heavy laden, and I will give you rest. Take My yoke upon you and learn from Me, for I am gentle and lowly in heart, and you will find rest for your souls. For My yoke is easy and My burden is light" *(Matthew 11:25b-30).*

Do you see the difference? It is so rewarding to see someone you have discipled receive great blessings after enduring the same tests and trials that you have come through yourself. These trials force you to increase your faith so you will be prepared to help lead others through their tough times of crises. We are to reach out and pull them from the water just as Jesus did for the apostle Peter. What if the Lord had counted all that He knew Peter would do in the future against him while he was sinking in the raging waters? It is easy to be a sideline referee, but let us remember that Peter was walking on the water when he cried out for help from his mentor. Peter only began to sink when his eyes turned away from his teacher. As soon as he cried out to Jesus, he was pulled back into the boat, and it moved instantly to the shoreline. Once again, Peter stood on solid ground with his master.

Jesus did not say to Peter, "Drown, you immature baby. You are actually going to deny me three times just at my most critical moments. Why should I waste any more time on you? I am tired of whining babies!" No—Jesus just reached out and pulled him in—revealing to us once again His unconditional love in action.

Please realize that new baby Christians will test us, and that is exactly why they are in our paths.

God designed it that way. Without the Lord Jesus it is humanly impossible to possess genuine unconditional love. Just as we are the children of the Lord, we are also someone's earthly children. In order to mentor others, we must first be mentored ourselves.

Have you ever noticed that the newer the Christian the more unconditional love seems to be present? Have you ever seen a brand new Christian walking into the church's group of "stalwart, card–carrying–believers–baptized–in–pickle–juice–club?"(PJC) Without even realizing it, the excited new Christian had bubbled enough around them to turn the "pickle juice club" (PJC) members' callused apple carts upside down. You can almost hear the PJC members thinking, "When will this baby settle down and come out of the clouds to the real world?" They forget that they were once that innocent-in-the-Lord-baby eons ago. What they do not realize is that in the baby's innocence, he or she is spiritually closer to the Kingdom of God and the Lord Jesus than they are in their self-righteousness.

"Assuredly, I say to you, whoever does not receive the kingdom of God as a little child will by no means enter it" (Luke 18:17).

We absolutely must remember that someone listened and cared for us as we excitedly saw our very nature become transformed. Our total desire base became "brand spanking new."

"Therefore, if anyone is in Christ, he is a new creation; old things have passed away; behold, all things have become new" (2 Corinthians 5:17).

We had to be excited because this was as big as life itself; we were brand new and for the first time alive in Christ Jesus. I have a sweet friend and adopted mom, Dr. Mary Ruth Swope, who taught me this: "Stay excited about your walk with Jesus. That is one of the secrets for staying in His presence!" I really believe that is one of the secrets of a Christian's success.

"And now abide faith, hope, love, these three; but the greatest of these is love." 1 Corinthians 13:13

"For God so loved the world that He gave His only begotten Son, that whoever believes in Him should not perish but have everlasting life." John 3:16

Chapter 6

Sin Bashers

Some churches are very guilty of being adamant sin-bashers in their fleshly attempts at righteousness. In doing so, they often crucify the sinner with the sin. The church must never condone sin but should first love the sinner.

I have been party to this "smugness revival" that develops with good intentions. I agreed with the many people that said God's judgment would fall upon certain regions of the world because they had a high tolerance for sin.

Did I really love and care for those sinners? Did I begin to pull down the strongholds of sin over that region during my prayer closet time? No—I judged them into hell and rinsed off my hands with the water of spiritual self-righteousness. After all, I was not one of them! Again, was the sinner right? No. Was I right? No. Who won? The devil always wins the self-righteousness game. Self-righteousness is derived from the spirit of pride, and the devil uses it as one of his most effective weapons. That is why Jesus Christ said our righteousness is as filthy rags.

"All of us have become like one who is unclean, and all our righteous acts are like filthy rags; we all shrivel up like a leaf, and like the wind our sins sweep us away" (Isaiah 64:6 NIV).

We should never placate the sin that is trying to destroy God's creation. I would rather we say, "Love the righteousness of the Lord so much through a lifestyle of God's unconditional love that hatred does not have to enter the picture. Thus, you will not have to live on a 'sanctimonious platform' as a Christian 'displaying a continuous hatred toward sin' with everyone you meet." I want to be transparent and see myself as God does. Also, I need to view myself as many others do in order to be the best possible witness of Jesus' unconditional love. Of course, I hate sin. So do you, if you are dedicated to Jesus Christ.

"Guard my life, for I am devoted to you. You are my God; save your servant who trusts in you. Have mercy on me, O Lord, for I call to You all day long. Bring joy to your servant, for to You, O Lord, I lift up my soul. You are forgiving and

good, O Lord, abounding in love to all who call to You. Hear my prayer, O LORD; listen to my cry for mercy. In the day of my trouble I will call to You, for You will answer me. Among the gods there is none like You, O Lord; no deeds can compare with Yours. All the nations You have made will come and worship before You, O Lord; they will bring glory to Your name. For You are great and do marvelous deeds; You alone are God. Teach me Your way, O LORD, and I will walk in Your truth; give me an undivided heart, that I may fear Your name" *(Psalms 86:2-11 NIV).*

The important thing is how we display our feelings while trying to show love to already lost and sinful people around us. Just ask yourself if you were a lost sinner, would you prefer more love, acceptance and forgiveness around you, or would you choose a venue of sin-bashing to surround you? Be careful not to ever get caught up in the trick of the enemy and take what you started out meaning for good to the extreme. You may find yourself picketing against sin, traveling down some rabbit-trail direction of life that no doubt had roots of meaningful purpose. An example is a preacher with a call to plant churches that gets caught up in the anti-abortion campaign. He then loses sight of the ministry to which God called him. Some misguided Christians have erred in even resorting to violence and blowing up doctor's clinics, killing yet more innocent lives while trying to protect unborn babies. Is God in that? No. I do not believe He is, nor does He condone that behavior. I, for one, literally detest abortion. The killing of unborn babies is murder, plain and simple. We will be judged for it. But I fast, pray and vote my convictions.

Somehow along the way many people have lost perspective of the lifestyle of unconditional love that Jesus modeled perfectly for us. Christians can easily bring judgment upon themselves in an effort to be righteous, especially if their efforts are approached in the flesh. *"Why? Because they did not seek it by faith, but as it were, by the works of the law. For they stumbled at that stumbling stone" (Romans 9:32).*

"And now abide faith, hope, love, these three; but the greatest of these is love." 1 Corinthians 13:13

"For God so loved the world that He gave His only begotten Son, that whoever believes in Him should not perish but have everlasting life." John 3:16

"And now abide faith, hope, love, these three;
but the greatest of these is love." 1 Corinthians 13:13

"For God so loved the world that He gave His only
begotten Son, that whoever believes in Him should
not perish but have everlasting life." John 3:16

Chapter 7

Are You a "Holy Joe" for JESUS?

Holiness is a matter of the heart and not of outward appearance. I will never forget being raised in a fundamental denomination that had a lengthy list of rules, or rather an unwritten code of conduct, for its membership based upon what you did not do. That is what mattered most.

Having just been called into the ministry, I was once refused permission by a pastor of one of the churches in this same denomination to minister in his church. When I asked why, the pastor said it was because my hair touched the tops of my ears. He said he had to protect his church, "as it was one that taught holiness."

Do you think that made me want to run down, get a "burr haircut," and dash back to him for his approval of me as holy? No, it actually saddened me as a new preacher and made me distance myself from him, thanking God that I was not caught up in such shallow teachings. When we approach God from the flesh, God will not acknowledge us, because flesh is carnal. Flesh and blood cannot inherit the Kingdom of God. Anytime we approach God in the flesh, we are working from our own perspective or from the outside in. God transforms us from the inside out.

"There is therefore now no condemnation to those who are in Christ Jesus, who do not walk according to the flesh, but according to the Spirit. For the law of the Spirit of life in Christ Jesus has made me free from the law of sin and death. For what the law could not do in that it was weak through the flesh, God did by sending His own Son in the likeness of sinful flesh, on account of sin: He condemned sin in the flesh, that the righteous requirement of the law might be fulfilled in us who do not walk according to the flesh but according to the Spirit.

"For those who live according to the flesh set their minds on the things of the flesh, but those who live according to the Spirit, the things of the Spirit. For to be carnally minded is death, but to be spiritually minded is life and peace. Because the carnal mind is enmity against God;

for it is not subject to the law of God, nor indeed can be.

"So then, those who are in the flesh cannot please God. But you are not in the flesh but in the Spirit, if indeed the Spirit of God dwells in you. Now if anyone does not have the Spirit of Christ, he is not His. And if Christ is in you, the body is dead because of sin, but the Spirit is life because of righteousness" (Romans 8:1-10).

Remember that Peter meant well in defending Jesus by cutting off the right ear of the high priest's slave with his sword during Christ's arrest in the garden of Gethsemane, *"And behold, one of those who were with Jesus reached and drew out his sword, and struck the slave of the high priest and cut off his ear" (Matthew 26:51 NASB).* Peter had not yet been transformed and restored spiritually by the Lord and the Holy

Spirit. He was operating in the same proud flesh that he did when he self-righteously snapped back to the Lord that he would never deny Him. Remember, the Sword of the Spirit and not the sword of flesh, wins victories for the Christian.

What did Jesus do? According to Luke's Gospel, Jesus instructed Peter to put away his sword and then performed a loving miracle by touching the ear of the high priest's slave and healing him. With evil intent they had come to arrest Jesus. Jesus never condemned nor returned evil for evil. Sin is sin, but love always prevails and covers a multitude of sins.

"And above all things have fervent love for one another, for love will cover a multitude of sins" (1 Peter 4:8).

"They think it strange that you do not run with them in the same flood of dissipation, speaking evil of you. They will give an account to Him who is ready to judge the living and the dead" (1 Peter 4:4-5 NIV).

"But I say to you who hear: Love your enemies, do good to those who hate you, bless those who curse you, and pray for those who spitefully use you" (Luke 6:27-28).

"And now abide faith, hope, love, these three;
but the greatest of these is love." 1 Corinthians 13:13

"For God so loved the world that He gave His only
begotten Son, that whoever believes in Him should
not perish but have everlasting life." John 3:16

"And now abide faith, hope, love, these three; but the greatest of these is love." 1 Corinthians 13:13

"For God so loved the world that He gave His only begotten Son, that whoever believes in Him should not perish but have everlasting life." John 3:16

Chapter 8

"Yardstick Christianity"

An example of how "Yardstick Christianity" is used by the enemy in an attempt to destroy lives is the sin of sexual perversion. The homosexual sinner did not sit at lunch one day and say, "Oh, today is a great day to forsake being a normal man or woman and to make a complete change in my lifestyle by adopting homosexuality." On the contrary, sinners bound by the sin of homosexuality are lost with no foundation of love to turn to without Jesus. Even if they have been raised in a church, they may have received rejection by a church group that used measurement indicators against people lost in sin. The church members may have categorized them by degrees, or "yardsticks," measuring them rather than unconditionally loving them as Jesus displayed. They may have been defending their flesh-born standards of holiness to a sinner who cannot identify with flesh and blood disguised as godliness. Sinners are the first to see right through their masks.

As a sinner continues in sin, he faces further rejection brought on by satan's plans and therefore becomes vulnerable to satan's lies. The devil's lies are causing the sinner to simply seek acceptance of their sin within satan's web. In the sin of homosexuality satan's web is "the gay life subculture." Thus, the sinner turns to satan's counterfeit desire for love and acceptance that ends up leading to total depravity of the person. Remember, you are not your own. Just as the Lord said you are bought with a price; satan has his price as well. Their sexual perversion caused them to become chained to a "depraved mind." The devil holds them captive and steals their freedom to live the normal Christian life. *"Furthermore, since they did not think it worthwhile to retain the knowledge of God, He gave them over to a depraved mind, to do what ought not to be done" (Romans 1:28 NIV).* Thus, they are trapped by a vicious sin-cycle, causing them to give up hope of ever finding freedom. They become as equally bound as the heroin addict who robs or kills for his next fix. Left to run its course, sin will ultimately destroy anyone. *"For the wages of sin is death..." (Romans 6:23a).* However, when a sinner who has reached bottom is crying out for help and reaching out to us, that person desperately needs to feel genuine unconditional love, acceptance and forgiveness.

Unfortunately, we have driven many "seeking sinners" to their grave of destruction because we became the Pharisee. We judged and sentenced them to eternity without Jesus. We did this with a "cloak of self-righteousness" and said it was exactly what they deserved. For another example of sexual sin where Jesus modeled unconditional love, one may look to the story of the men who brought the woman who had been caught in the very act of adultery to Jesus. In contrast to judgmental and self-righteous comments, Jesus lovingly said to the woman caught in adultery, *"...where are those accusers of yours? Has no one condemned you?...Neither do I condemn you; go and sin no more" (John 8:10b-11b).*

"Then the scribes and Pharisees brought to Him a woman caught in adultery. And when they

had set her in the midst, they said to Him, 'Teacher, this woman was caught in adultery, in the very act. Now Moses, in the law, commanded us that such should be stoned. But what do You say?' This they said, testing Him, that they might have something of which to accuse Him. But Jesus stooped down and wrote on the ground with His finger, as though He did not hear. So when they continued asking Him, He raised Himself up and said to them, 'He who is without sin among you, let him throw a stone at her first.' And again He stooped down and wrote on the ground. Then those who heard it, being convicted by their conscience, went out one by one, beginning with the oldest even to the last. And Jesus was left alone, and the woman standing in the midst. When Jesus had raised Himself up and saw no one but the woman, He said to her, 'Woman, where are those accusers of yours? Has no one condemned you?' She *said, 'No one, Lord.' And Jesus said to her, 'Neither do I condemn you; go and sin no more.' Then Jesus spoke to them again, saying, 'I am the light of the world. He who follows Me shall not walk in darkness, but have the light of life'" (John 8:3-12).*

There are consequences to sin. They come as a product of sowing and reaping, but we need to have no boundaries as Christians in loving sinners unconditionally. I would much rather see gay people saved and living for the Lord if they are dying of AIDS than to leave them in the clutches of satan's grip without hope of an eternity with the Lord. It is entirely better though if these people receive complete healing from the Lord. Love always endures and prevails.

"It is the same way for the resurrection of the dead. Our earthly bodies, which die and decay, will be different when they are resurrected, for

they will never die. Our bodies now disappoint us, but when they are raised, they will be full of glory. They are weak now, but when they are raised, they will be full of power. They are natural human bodies now, but when they are raised, they will be spiritual bodies. For just as there are natural bodies, so also there are spiritual bodies" (1 Corinthians 15:42-44 NLT).

A touching example of how God's love prevails is portrayed in the movie *The End of the Spear*. Members of the Waodani tribe of Ecuador brutally speared five missionaries (including Nate Saint and Jim Elliot) to death on January 8, 1956. Soon after this, Nate Saint's sister Rachel and his son moved into the jungle of Ecuador to share the love and forgiveness of Jesus. Also, Jim Elliot's widow Elizabeth came and stayed with the dwindling Waodani tribe for some time to show them God's great love. Miraculously, after so many years of retaining such hatred and fear within themselves, the Waodani tribe received the unconditional love of God. This tribe then started growing, flourishing and enjoying the many blessings of the Lord. Now the converted tribe of over 2,000 members has "adopted" Steve Saint, the son of the missionary they brutally speared to death and lovingly call him "Grandfather." Steve Saint (who was only 9 years old when his father was killed) has spent many summers in Ecuador since then, sharing the love of Jesus. This is such a wonderful example of God's unconditional love, acceptance and forgiveness in action.

"Do not seek revenge or bear a grudge against one of your people, but love your neighbor as yourself. I am the LORD" (Leviticus 19:18 NIV).

"And now abide faith, hope, love, these three; but the greatest of these is love." 1 Corinthians 13:13

"For God so loved the world that He gave His only begotten Son, that whoever believes in Him should not perish but have everlasting life." John 3:16

"And now abide faith, hope, love, these three; but the greatest of these is love." 1 Corinthians 13:13

"For God so loved the world that He gave His only begotten Son, that whoever believes in Him should not perish but have everlasting life." John 3:16

Chapter 9

By the Gift of God's Grace

"...but the gift of God is eternal life in Christ Jesus our Lord" (Romans 6:23b). God has a remedy if someone wants or needs deliverance. Jesus Christ of Nazareth said in John 6:37b KJV, *"...and him that cometh to Me I will in no wise cast out."*

Remember, humans create conditions of salvation from the outward appearance. God never does.

Instead, He looks at the heart. We should not excuse ourselves from small sins just because we feel we are not guilty of more serious ones. Blasphemy against the Holy Spirit, which is the unpardonable sin, is extremely serious but God makes it clear that He hates all sin. Sin is sin. *"If we say that we have no sin, we deceive ourselves, and the truth is not in us. If we confess our sins, He is faithful and just to forgive us our sins and to cleanse us from all unrighteousness. If we say that we have not sinned, we make Him a liar, and His word is not in us. My little children, these things I write to you, so that you may not sin. And if anyone sins, we have an Advocate with the Father, Jesus Christ the righteous. And He Himself is the propitiation for our sins, and not for ours only but also for the whole world"* (1 John 1:8-2:2). We are all guilty of sin because all of us have fallen short at one time or another. *"for all have sinned and fall short of the glory of God, being justified freely by His grace through the redemption that is in Christ Jesus, whom God set forth as a propitiation by His blood, through faith, to demonstrate His righteousness, because in His forbearance God had passed over the sins that were previously committed, to demonstrate at the present time His righteousness, that He might be just and the justifier of the one who has faith in Jesus" (Romans 3:23-26).* Some people may think the sin of complaining is not as bad as other sins like adultery or murder, but it says in God's Word that murmuring or complaining displeases God. *"Through Jesus, therefore, let us continually offer to God a sacrifice of praise—the fruit of lips that confess his name" (Hebrews 13:15 NIV).*

Complaining about God's will for our lives can result in stubbornness or rebellion. Rebellion is as the sin of witchcraft so we must not allow the devil to deceive us into running from or fighting against the Lord's will for our lives. *"For rebellion is as the sin of witchcraft, and stubbornness is as iniquity and idolatry..." (1 Samuel 15:23a).* We must not allow satan to deceive us into compromising with little white lies, small exaggerations or even complaining. Almighty God is holy, and any sin causes separation from Him. Sin ultimately causes excruciating pain and sometimes even death. This is why we must repent daily and keep a "contrite and humble heart."

"For thus says the High and Lofty One Who inhabits eternity, Whose name is Holy: 'I dwell in the high and holy place, with him who has a contrite and humble spirit, to revive the spirit of the humble, and to revive the heart of the contrite ones'" (Isaiah 57:15). We must allow the Lord to change and transform us from within.

"So rend your heart, and not your garments; return to the LORD your God, for He is gracious and merciful, slow to anger, and of great kindness; and He relents from doing harm" (Joel 2:13).

At times we have lived the lies of the world, as mentioned briefly in the example about the "compromised lifestyle," by conditioning everything in life from the outside in. Our lives always crumble if there is no inner foundation. We must gain this foundation, which must come from both the knowledge and understanding of Jesus' love for His own. This faith foundation is also gained by accepting Jesus at His Word.

Why do we make such distinctions between the "up and out" as opposed to the "down and out?" Although many Christians will not admit it, they do this, also. Why? I believe it is because our flesh and our pride tell us the "up and out" will be much easier to approach and far more beneficial to our cause once reached than the "down and out" would ever be. That distinction and decision to minister primarily to the "up and out" is derived from a base of religious flesh principle that asks, "Ultimately, what is in it for me?" or "How can ministering to the 'down and out' end up benefiting my platform or my success?" To illustrate, let me cite just one example of the hundreds available.

Some people will jump in quickly to assist in the work at churches rather than go out and minister to the homeless or gays in downtown areas such as San Francisco or other places. However, one report of this type of ministry comes from a couple of young men dedicated to taking the Gospel to the lost in the inner city of San Francisco. They testified that after ministering to one young man who was lost in the pits of sin in this culture, they saw him miraculously delivered. Then they found out his father was a wealthy CEO of one of the nation's largest banks. The story goes that the young man's father was so elated that his son had been rescued from the pits of hell, that he committed to financially sowing funds back into the inner-city ministry that had dared to be obedient in the rescue of his son. Who would ever have thought that by being obedient to God's commandments to the "uttermost," one would see this kind of financial reward to help win the "gutter-most?"

It just goes to show that we cannot judge a "pearl of great price" by its outward appearance. So, whether up, down or lost; lost is still lost. Let us take a lesson from the Lord Jesus and simply be obedient by displaying love unconditionally wherever He takes us.

Jesus wants desperately to be your Savior. Thus, He wants all the kingdoms of your heart. Once He has your heart completely, He is your life. Then, without even trying, you will look up one day, as I did, and realize you are not your own, and your total desire base will be transformed to the deeper things of God. The very essence of this message to all of us is that we are called to love sinners unconditionally. You are not in control of designing your every move. As a believer you are allowing the creator to guide your life, and you are now simply the "loving meal server" offering up life—and life more abundantly—to those in need. That is why the sinners may want to be around you. Not because you have impressed them, but rather that the Christ in you has loved them into a "family of divine belonging." Everyone wants to belong to the beloved, even the hermit and the loner. They just disguise it in a different way.

We were created to love and worship God. We will worship something. So satan deceives many to turn that worship to him. That is all the more reason we must live the model of unconditional love for as many souls as possible.

Some people try everything in the flesh. So did the Scribes and Pharisees in Jesus' day. All those extremely religious leaders, who chose not to follow Jesus, protected their own lifestyles. They insulated themselves in their *"...whitewashed tombs which indeed appear beautiful outwardly, but inside are full of dead men's bones and all uncleanness" (Matthew 23:27b).* Rather than the love of fellow man, called "saving grace," they had a ministry of "saving face." Finding fault with the revelation message of the day from Jesus Christ, they sought after Him to lure Him into a web to try to ultimately make Him look unfounded in truth. Christ's obedient love cut right to the heart of their self-righteous fleshly kingdoms. Jesus revealed their foundations and motives, which were based upon works of the flesh.

God does not require rigid religious practices from us, rather a daily repentance, continual intimacy and fellowship with Him. You see, once the Lord draws us to Himself and reigns in every kingdom of our heart, we will truly experience unconditional love. Whether the catalyst for our conversion was a crisis or not, if we truly repent and find what it is like to have Jesus Christ as complete Lord of our lives, then we will experience His amazing love and the joy of His presence.

You should not expect your former worldly family to accept the "new person" you have become. You are a new creation in Christ Jesus, and your desires have totally changed. Do not wait on your personal invitation back into the same circles. On the contrary, you may want to write a few courtesy notes explaining how the Lord radically transformed your life and that you are no longer the same person. Not that you really want to keep spending time with your old circle of friends; they may just need to hear from you to witness where you stand. You should keep reaching out to them from time to time for an opportunity to love them unconditionally, but if they do not respond positively, never let their non-responsiveness hurt your feelings. This is the way the Lord separates light from darkness.

The Lord never became a friend to the world in order to win it. Jesus is the Savior for all sinners, and He loves them unconditionally. Yet, Christ never compromised the truth of His heavenly Father, Almighty God, to belong to a family of sinners. He was non-condemning around them, but His disciples were actually His intimate friends. Remember, the Lord said in Matthew 10:34-36 KJV, *"Think not that I am come to send peace on earth: I came not to send peace, but a sword. For I am come to set a man at variance against his father, and the daughter against her mother, and the daughter in law against her mother in law. And a man's foes shall be they of his own household."* Jesus' disciples actually became His real family on earth.

If you ever see your former friends from the sinful world where you once belonged, you may experience the feeling of a "painful distance" as you get a glimpse of your "old person." This pain is used by the Holy Spirit to remind you that the greatest measure of sadness is to be lost without hope of Jesus' love. Like the father of the prodigal son said in Luke 15:24 KJV, *"For this my son was dead, and is alive again; he was lost and is found…."*

Your new spiritual family will respect you because they know to whom you truly belong. On the other hand, even though your former circle of friends may respect your choice, it is just an unwritten rule that they will think you have gone off the "deep-end" with religion. It was the same during the introduction of Christianity to the early church and has never changed. To your former Pharisees or lost friends, you have become a fanatic. Your once close-knit peers wrongly view such a heart transformation as showing instability and weakness. Even though the former friends know the truth deep down inside, they work desperately to protect their carnal kingdoms. Nevertheless, people must decide for themselves. You cannot make their decisions.

However, you can show unconditional love by praying for them fervently.

You can be sure the "Sanhedrin" of the "First Nominal Country Club Church" will do everything in their power to shatter your loving spiritual experience if given the opportunity. One way they like to do so is by telling you and others as much as possible about the "real you they knew in your sin condition" with the fleshly motive to discredit you as a person of unstable character. They may think it is to their benefit to seize any opportunity to "rake you over the coals" while by chance associating with your new spiritual family. Do not take this personally and allow the devil to use it as one of his shards to spear your new abundant life in the Lord. This is only the devil working through people who do not really know the Lord intimately. In actuality, they take such actions as a means for marking their platform boundaries of support in order to assure that they are not losing ground to the "fanatical world of freedom in Christ." In the end, on Judgment Day, all people will give an account for their actions—period.

"But I say to you that for every idle word men may speak, they will give account of it in the day of judgment" (Matthew 12:36).

"Talk no more so very proudly; let no arrogance come from your mouth, for the LORD is the God of knowledge; and by Him actions are weighed" (1 Samuel 2:3).

During my days in the compromised camp, I would hear them talk about a newly "Born Again Believer," especially one who received the baptism of the Holy Spirit, that "He must have been in a real 'pickle' to run that hard toward fanaticism." Then they would nobly resound that it "would help him for now during his crisis, and he will settle back down after a bit. Let us just give him time to catch his balance." The devil equates words like "balance" and "moderation" with the "compromised camp."

Most of the time Spirit-filled Christians are actually well balanced, yet the enemy is constantly trying to weave ways to discredit fundamental believers.

One only has to glance at the way Hollywood often portrays Christian believers and ministers as the brunt of the jokes or the out-of-step, less intelligent people in many movies. The enemy supremely enjoys capitalizing on such cases, especially when a prominent believer or televangelist with lots of national exposure happens to fall. This is like offering hand-grenades to the "camp of the Pharisees," giving credence to their sacred earthly kingdom. The Lord never looked to the sanctimonious Pharisee sect for approval. His timely messages of razor-sharpened words of reformation constantly cut their hearts "to the quick." They were the ones who were hurt the most by Jesus exposing the truth about them. Jesus came to reveal and remove the works of flesh. The Pharisees and Sadducees were His greatest opposition, and it is the same spirit of anti-Christ that they possessed that tries to deny the Lordship of Jesus today. The spirit of anti-Christ will try to crucify both you as a believer and new believers as well. That is why all of satan's forces tried to keep Jesus Christ from defeating them. This could not stop the greatest act of unconditional love ever for God's own, "victory on the Cross of Calvary," where Jesus did ultimately defeat the devil forever. Now the devil has a short time frame to try to take with him every soul he can to his doom of eternal damnation. But God wills that none should perish but all have eternal life through Jesus Christ our Lord! *"Even so it is not the will of your Father who is in heaven that one of these little ones should perish"* *(Matthew 18:14).*

"And this is the will of Him who sent Me, that everyone who sees the Son and believes in Him may have everlasting life; and I will raise him up at the last day" (John 6:40).

There was a constant spiritual war raging from the extreme religious sects who hoped to get rid of this unconventional Jesus of Nazareth, who was teaching a new radical love Gospel. We still have spiritual battles today, only now we have the weapon that won the war present with us. We have the precious Blood of Jesus as an eternal sacrifice for our sins. He gave us this sacrifice with unconditional love. It defeated satan then, and it will do the same today. Jesus gave it to us saying, *"This is My commandment, that ye love one another, as I have loved you. Greater love hath no man than this, that a man lay down his life for his friends" (John 15:12-13 KJV).*

It is a trick of the enemy to get Christians drawn into fighting their battles against sin in the natural or flesh. That is exactly why Jesus gave us the commandment to love one another, and it is impossible to accomplish this without Him. Therefore, when Jesus hung upon that cross of humiliation and shame, before all who thought they had won, He cried out once and for all, *"It is finished!"*

"After this, Jesus, knowing that all things were now accomplished, that the Scripture might be fulfilled, said, 'I thirst!' Now a vessel full of

sour wine was sitting there; and they filled a sponge with sour wine, put it on hyssop, and put it to His mouth. So when Jesus had received the sour wine, He said, 'It is finished!' And bowing His head, He gave up His spirit" (John 19:28-30).

Thus, Jesus Christ won the victory over all the satanic works of the flesh. The Apostle Paul describes it best in Colossians 2:15 KJV, *"And having spoiled principalities and powers, He made a shew of them openly, triumphing over them in it."*

Romans 12:9 sounds a bit paradoxical when it says, *"Let love be without hypocrisy. Abhor what is evil. Cling to what is good."* You should not run from a verbal opportunity to share Jesus. Yet in order to reach many, you have to live the life of unconditional love by example, giving assistance whenever life's crises befall the lost or others in need. That is when we are called by God to be the "messenger of golden opportunity." We can be sure we will have crises, but where some sufferers are humbled and seek help during such tragedies, others are too bound by pride and satan's clutches to let go. Nonetheless, whether we ever see them at the point of need, their lack of the abundant life represents enough need on its own.

We should be careful not to fall into satan's trap with the self-righteous religious groups who cheer when their enemy stumbles. Yes, we often become their enemy as we receive and enjoy our freedom in the Lord. The bound religious people do not like to see us free at all and often attempt to hinder our forward progress in the Lord's service or stifle the ministry. That is when we truly have an opportunity to show absolute love.

The world system "shoots its wounded!" We must not let that religious spirit creep into our hearts or the church. We must pray, fast and decree the freedom of the Lord Jesus. We are free from the law, and once we are free, we are free indeed! *"Therefore if the Son makes you free, you shall be free indeed" (John 8:36).*

"And now abide faith, hope, love, these three; but the greatest of these is love." 1 Corinthians 13:13

"For God so loved the world that He gave His only begotten Son, that whoever believes in Him should not perish but have everlasting life." John 3:16

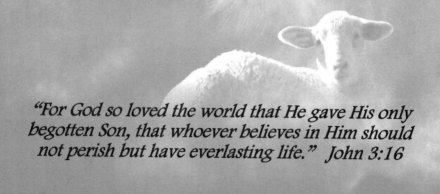

"And now abide faith, hope, love, these three;
but the greatest of these is love." 1 Corinthians 13:13

"For God so loved the world that He gave His only
begotten Son, that whoever believes in Him should
not perish but have everlasting life." John 3:16

Chapter 10

Abandon the Old; Put on the New

Do we mentally draw a dichotomy between the unconditional love of Jesus and man's approach to be a good person? Man's way desires only a form of goodness through any type of belief system. No matter what the belief system, we cannot know and be accepted by God without accepting Jesus Christ as our Lord and Savior. This is the one premise that it all boils down to, but more often many people will not admit they want it their way rather than God's way. It was no different in the early days of the world, as was evidenced through God's dealings with His chosen people. In the first of the Ten Commandments God addressed this: ***"Thou shalt have no other gods before me" (Deuteronomy 5:7).***

God's approach to reveal and transform the works of the flesh never starts with the flesh—rather, it starts with the heart, or the spirit of man. The spirit of a person has the God-given will to make a free-moral choice. We can be sure that it will always cost us something to make that choice. Sure, salvation is free; nevertheless, it comes with a price.

However, Jesus paid the supreme price, and thus ours is really a privilege rather than a price. Do you remember the story of the rich young man who wanted to follow Jesus as told in Luke 18:18-24? After he told Jesus he had kept all the commandments since his youth, Jesus said he still lacked one thing. The Lord said, ***"...Sell all that you have and distribute to the poor, and you will have treasure in heaven; and come, follow Me"*** ***(Luke 18:22b).***

If God had wanted man's salvation to be simply dependent upon how man succeeded in keeping all the commandments, then He never would have sent His only begotten Son into the world to redeem lost mankind to Himself.

Today, we are so blessed to have God's Word spoken to us in the complete Bible, something the early believers of Jesus' day did not have. Even though we do not have the privilege of living near Jesus in person as the early believers had while

He was on earth, we still have His Word and Holy Spirit to guide us.

"This Book of the Law shall not depart from your mouth, but you shall meditate in it day and night, that you may observe to do according to all that is written in it. For then you will make your way prosperous, and then you will have good success" (Joshua 1:8).

Jesus Christ entered into an extremely religious world, yet modeled for us and for those of His day unconditional love by imparting Himself totally into a group of disciples who were common representatives of the day. Did all who began to accept Him eagerly stay with Him? No. Some turned and went back to their old lifestyles of comfortable religious traditions. We know the rest of the story; the extremely religious leaders of Christ's day were the ones who had Jesus crucified. However, it was all in the ultimate plan of Almighty God. We need to bear in mind that God has a plan, and He never says, "Oops!" We serve a mighty and powerful, omniscient God. He is the great I AM, the Beginning and the End. *"This is what the LORD says—your Redeemer, the Holy One of Israel: 'I am the LORD your God, who teaches you what is best for you, who directs you in the way you should go'" (Isaiah 48:17 NIV).*

Our Creator does not make mistakes, but we surely do. God uses these mistakes for our good. When we call something a mistake, He says it is His divine purpose. As difficult as it is for our finite minds to fully comprehend the Word of God, it holds all truth for our lives. *"And we know that all things work together for good to those who Love God, to those who are the called according to His purpose" (Romans 8:28).*

"But God demonstrates His own love toward us, in that while we were still sinners, Christ died for us" (Romans 5:8).

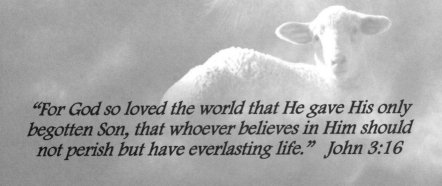

"And now abide faith, hope, love, these three;
but the greatest of these is love." 1 Corinthians 13:13

"For God so loved the world that He gave His only
begotten Son, that whoever believes in Him should
not perish but have everlasting life." John 3:16

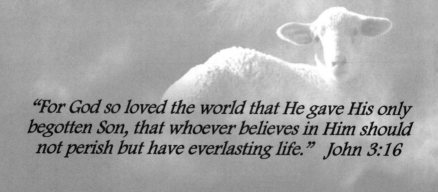

"And now abide faith, hope, love, these three; but the greatest of these is love." 1 Corinthians 13:13

"For God so loved the world that He gave His only begotten Son, that whoever believes in Him should not perish but have everlasting life." John 3:16

Chapter 11

Learn by Our Example—JESUS

Old slew-foot is crafty. If you are not on your toes, he will give you marching orders for how to do the work of the Lord in the flesh or even abandon it completely. Remember how satan gave the rich young ruler marching orders for abandoning the work of the Lord. This person had a love for money and stinginess in his heart. This resulted in his marching back home without giving up any of his wealth. He was unable to serve the Lord since Jesus gave the rich young ruler a prerequisite to follow Him; the young man went away sad, pondering the cost required for following Jesus, but unable to accept it. As the Word clearly shows us in Mark 10:19-23, ***"Then Jesus, looking at him, loved him, and said to him, 'One thing you lack: Go your way, sell whatever you have and give to the poor, and you will have treasure in heaven; and come, take up the cross, and follow Me.' But he was sad at this word, and went away sorrowful, for he had great possessions. Then Jesus looked around and said to His disciples, 'How hard it is for those who have riches to enter the kingdom of God!'"***

It seemed satan had won at least temporarily, but we do not know if the rich young man ever thought this through and finally one day sold all he had, gave it to the poor and followed after the Lord's teachings. The Bible does not say any more about him.

Nonetheless, notice that Jesus did not pursue the rich young ruler for the rest of His ministry on earth. There was not a new movement of His day called "Pursuing the Rich Young Rulers." Jesus simply shared the truth in love and continued His mission on earth. Jesus did have other things to do for the Father and was obedient in doing them. He did not have time to waste the rest of His days on earth chasing after this rich young ruler.

The point is that many Christians fall into the trap of wasting their precious ministry time "majoring on the minors." We often allow the enemy to use people who require us to spend 80 percent of our time on 20 percent of the problems. Those people need to devote their own time and energy to solve their problems and learn from their mistakes. Bear in mind that satan would love to trap us into getting bogged down sorting out all the debates of the vacillating, problematic Christians. Many are following after religion while chasing greener pastures instead of seeking growth and maturity in the Lord. Therefore, we would have little or no time for witnessing to the lost in our circle of influence if we allowed distractions from our calling of reaching the lost at any cost.

If we are following Jesus' model and abandoning any distractions to our calling, we are simply to love lost people to the point of having them receive and accept Jesus Christ as their personal Savior. In addition, we are to assist in their birthing process and help mentor them to maturity in the Kingdom of God. We are responsible for plugging them into a solid Christian discipleship group. If we do not have one to recommend, we need to start one.

However, new Christians need to accept some responsibility for their spiritual growth themselves. They can ask others to receive them into a Bible study or small home group to experience the powerful cleansing and joy of the Word of God. Also, this small group study will help them grow in the wisdom and knowledge of the Lord. *"The fear of the LORD is the beginning of wisdom, and the knowledge of the Holy One is understanding" (Proverbs 9:10).*

Nevertheless, when either a new Christian or someone who has known the Lord for a while still drifts in and out of different groups or churches, complaining constantly and/or creating daily problems, they cannot be allowed to monopolize all our ministry time. Such Christians tend to vacillate and demand our constant attention. They self-inflict wounds and ignore continued loving discipleship. Now, does that mean we are advocating a limited love and devotion to the unstable member? On the contrary, we are actually showing the true meaning of unconditional love by occasionally not helping. Sometimes the best help for people is to release them to let them help themselves.

We are allowing those people to grow by making right or wrong choices for themselves. They now have a level of knowledge, so they are responsible to the Lord. Does that sound like love? Did the Lord ever rebuke His own? Did the Lord ever allow His disciples to make mistakes? It seemed at times that all they did was make mistakes. Love is not always holding others' hands and telling them all they are doing is just fine, especially if it is not. Sometimes "the truth in love" spoken kindly is better for others and can be much more loving than taking the non-confrontational approach. In His perfect timing, Jesus always spoke "the truth in love," if appropriate and it was God's will. Rather than just holding others' hands and trying to make them feel better, we should simply assign ourselves to daily and weekly fervent prayer for them. We should also consider making phone calls, followed up by notes and inquiries of genuine unconditional love and concern when appropriate.

However, we cannot allow this person to alter our primary ministry focus so that we are less productive for the Lord. This may be perceived by some as indifference. However, it has been my experience that those who persist in this perception are majoring in religious traditions rather than the ministry of "unconditional love for the lost." Genuine love develops not from our intellect, nor from romantic depictions we see projected on the motion picture screen, but from the innermost feelings of our hearts and spirits. An example is found in Luke 10:41-42, of Mary and Martha, who had Jesus as a guest at Martha's house. Martha was the really busy one concerned with practical matters, and Mary took the time to sit at Jesus' feet and pour out her devoted "agape love" to Him as she listened intently to her Lord.

"And Jesus answered and said to her, 'Martha, Martha, you are worried and troubled about many things. But one thing is needed, and Mary has chosen that good part, which will not be taken away from her'" (Luke 10:41-42).

"Busyness" of ministry is not always the most productive for the Lord. The "fruit" in a Christian's life seems always to be the genuine evidence of "Being in His Presence." We must love the Lord our God with everything in us!

That is why there is not a better time or setting for this ministry of unconditional love than in the small and intimate home group modeled for us by Jesus. Just as He was lovingly reminding Martha that her sister had chosen the good part that would not be taken away from her, He introduced this to us for a reason. The church today has a guide that has never been changed by Jesus. We have made many alterations, yet returning to this example is of paramount importance in order to fulfill His pattern for evangelism and discipleship. Christ spent most of His time in close-knit personal group settings in various homes displaying unconditional love to His disciples and people that He wanted to use as examples of God's love. When some people complained about Jesus' demonstration of unconditional love to sinners *"...He said to them, 'Those who are well have no need of a physician, but those who are sick'"* *(Matthew 9:12b).*

Once you truly experience and grasp the significance of a small group ministry, you soon realize it is necessary in order to accomplish His commandment feasibly to *"...make disciples of all nations..." (Matthew 28:19).*

"And now abide faith, hope, love, these three; but the greatest of these is love." 1 Corinthians 13:13

"For God so loved the world that He gave His only begotten Son, that whoever believes in Him should not perish but have everlasting life." John 3:16

"And now abide faith, hope, love, these three;
but the greatest of these is love." 1 Corinthians 13:13

"For God so loved the world that He gave His only
begotten Son, that whoever believes in Him should
not perish but have everlasting life." John 3:16

Chapter 12

Keep Your Eyes on the LORD

God will not share His glory with anyone: not man, not angels that tried to be like God nor anyone that wants to be his own selfish god. The devil tries to present himself as a selfish god. Never forget that satan was the highest angel at one time. Do not think he will not keep trying to get you to remove your eyes from the Lord, your family and your ministry to put those fleshly eyes upon yourself. That is his job. He goes about it daily because he has a chip on his shoulder, knowing that he fell and is eternally defeated. *"It is written: 'As surely as I live,' says the Lord, 'every knee will bow before me; every tongue will confess to God'"* *(Romans 14:11 NIV)*.

"He will be great, and will be called the Son of the Highest; and the Lord God will give Him the throne of His father David. And He will reign over the house of Jacob forever, and of His kingdom there will be no end" (Luke 1:32-33).

"Therefore God also has highly exalted Him and given Him the name which is above every name, that at the name of Jesus every knee should bow, of those in heaven, and of those on earth, and of those under the earth, and that every tongue should confess that Jesus Christ is

Lord, to the glory of God the Father" *(Philippians 2:9-11).*

The devil wants to kill, steal and destroy as many as he can before he is engulfed into that eternal lake of fire and damnation that was, by the way, designed only for him, the fallen angels and satan's followers. Humans were created in the image of God. *"So God created man in His own image; in the image of God He created him; male and female He created them" (Genesis 1:27).* When we choose to be smug and live a veneer of self-righteous religion, we are actually saying to the lost who live within our circle of influence, "We do not care where you go!"

"The thief does not come except to steal, and to kill, and to destroy. I have come that they may have life, and that they may have it more abundantly" (John 10:10).

One day it finally dawned on me that I outwardly appeared to be a Christian but had evolved into a "card-carrying hypocrite" who had lost my first love and developed a throne in my kingdom to honor myself. The Lord spoke to me sternly about this just as He did to His chosen people, the children of Israel. God made it clear to His people that He will not tolerate man's attempt to combine Him with their compromised lifestyle. They compromised their lives and then listened to the false prophets of their day. God sent the true Prophet Ezekiel as a messenger to warn them that these false prophets were "tickling their ears" by saying just what they wanted to hear.

Read what God said to Israel in Ezekiel 13:4-9 KJV. *"O Israel, thy prophets are like the foxes in the deserts. Ye have not gone up into the gaps, neither made up the hedge for the house of Israel to stand in the battle in the day of the*

LORD. They have seen vanity and lying divination, saying, The LORD saith: and the LORD hath not sent them: and they have made others to hope that they would confirm the word. Have ye not seen a vain vision, and have ye not spoken a lying divination, whereas ye say, The LORD saith it; albeit I have not spoken? Therefore thus saith the Lord GOD; Because ye have spoken vanity, and seen lies, therefore, behold, I am against you, saith the Lord GOD. And mine hand shall be upon the prophets that see vanity, and that divine lies: they shall not be in the assembly of my people, neither shall they be written in the writing of the house of Israel, neither shall they enter into the land of Israel; and ye shall know that I am the Lord GOD."

Do you see that the Lord does not hesitate to chasten His chosen people? How can we play such games with God? Do we think we will get by with our own plans, constructing and ruling the kingdoms in our hearts before an Almighty God? Why? The following are the reasons we may answer the questions incorrectly:

1. The lack of knowledge of the Living God
2. The lack of the fear of God

In the past my answers were based mostly on ignorance as I did not know God well enough, realistically, to fear and respect Him. Even though I was professing to do so, I did not really know the Father by first loving Him with all my heart, my mind and my soul. Do we really know God the Father? It is His Son we can know and through Him know the Father.

Whatever the cause, there is not any excuse that will stand up to God on the Day of Judgment. Even if I stood before Almighty God and said, "Lord, those false prophets made me believe I was just fine in my 'First Nominal Church' " or

"I just did the best I could while doing it my way and listening to them placate my conscience," there would still be no adequate excuse. Somehow, I remembered hearing the Bible verse in Matthew 25:41 that says, ***"Then He will also say to those on the left hand, 'Depart from Me, you cursed, into the everlasting fire prepared for the devil and his angels.'"***

God makes it clear to ***"...choose for yourselves this day whom you will serve..." (Joshua 24:15).*** You cannot serve both the kingdom of self and the Kingdom of God. ***"Jesus knew their thoughts and said to them, 'Every kingdom divided against itself will be ruined, and every city or household divided against itself will not stand'" (Matthew 12:25).***

The former angel satan and his fallen angels have always tried to tempt God and undermine the entire plan set forth by Almighty God. The devil tries at every turn to abort God's plan. Remember, that is satan's sole objective. The devil knows his time is ticking and is like a madman with nothing to lose. Yet we know he has already lost, because Jesus has the Victory!

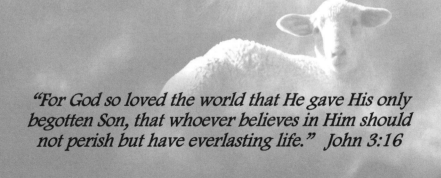

"And now abide faith, hope, love, these three; but the greatest of these is love." 1 Corinthians 13:13

"For God so loved the world that He gave His only begotten Son, that whoever believes in Him should not perish but have everlasting life." John 3:16

"And now abide faith, hope, love, these three; but the greatest of these is love." *1 Corinthians 13:13*

"For God so loved the world that He gave His only begotten Son, that whoever believes in Him should not perish but have everlasting life." *John 3:16*

Chapter 13

Idolatry Today?

God is Love. He only wanted closeness and fellowship with His creation. He had a plan to love and fellowship with each of us from the beginning.

Sin always came to man in the form of many deceptions. For so many lost people, this deceptive sin is the "idol of self." By infiltrating the arts, satan has handed us many nasty deceptions. The song from days past, *I Did It My*

Way comes to mind. I can remember listening so proudly in my lost condition to those "kingdoms of flesh" messages, boldly sung from many different artists.

Everyone that listened, purchased, and viewed this and any other "idol of self" art also contributed to its popularity. This art's negative effect on the minds and hearts of many people is still prevalent today and has caused an even further acceleration of the "idol of self" mentality. This reverberates even louder than that when we consider how man consistently tries to be the captain of his own ship, though he was never created to be!

God is the creator and captain of our ship. We may plan our steps, but God directs our paths. ***"In his heart a man plans his course, but the***

LORD determines his steps" (Proverbs 16:9 NIV).

There are wonderful people who live a life transformed from sin, but many of those have been taught a graduated scale of compromise. It often happens that "The First Church of Programmed Christianity" tries to heap on double and triple scoops of divine insulation to pad us from the monster we were when Jesus originally saved us. Then, if we remain in such a compromised lifestyle, we may end up unfulfilled either by overdosing on "spiritual bless-me food," or even worse, thinking we are just fine when we are not.

The devil tries to prevent us from being a blessing to others any possible way he can. If we attended a Christian crusade every week, we would be worn-out spiritual seekers affecting very few lost people for the sake of the Kingdom of God. We would have little fruit to show for our "hyper-spiritualized" Christian life. How can attending church services and functions, revivals, crusades or conferences every single night of the week be a compromise in our Christian walk? Love God, not just God's stuff! Just because we go to all this "churchy stuff" does not mean we are really there, completely loving God with all our heart, soul and mind. Most importantly, though, it does not mean that we are being obedient to Him. If we are too busy doing just what we think is spiritually gratifying, then we will be unable to hear from the Lord God for our correct instructions to take us to the destiny He has prepared for us. It is important that we are available to the Lord and follow his Word, taking care of all our responsibilities. We must only go where He tells us to go, say only what He tells us to say and do just what is pleasing to our

Heavenly Father. *"I delight to do Your will, O my God, And Your law is within my heart"* *(Psalms 40:8).*

"And now abide faith, hope, love, these three; but the greatest of these is love." 1 Corinthians 13:13

"For God so loved the world that He gave His only begotten Son, that whoever believes in Him should not perish but have everlasting life." John 3:16

Chapter 14

Is Being Blessed Always Best?

Understand that compromise is still compromise. The world's compromise that kept you from Almighty God will certainly come in as an angel of light anytime if it is possible to keep you on the "comfy church pew cushion." *"And no wonder! For satan himself transforms himself into an angel of light" (2 Corinthians 11:14).* The devil tries to keep us stagnant rather than serving the Lord Jesus by witnessing and fulfilling our destiny of ministry to hurting and lost people. Many people live the "churchy scene" that meets on Sunday mornings but do nothing during the main ministry week that goes from Monday through Saturday. I totally believe in edifying the person and building up one another in the Lord. I just do not believe a denomination within your walk of Christianity needs to be developed around that premise. If we take in more blessings than we give out in ministry, we get a "moldy manna mentality." Quite simply, if the blessing flow is always heading toward us, our focus becomes inward and out of balance.

On the other hand, an outward focus will give us many more opportunities to share unconditional love with so many people. Then we can share the love of Jesus with an intimate group that has ongoing values and responsibilities with one another. Also, we stay focused on the mission of lost people in our spheres of influence. We call that "accountability" in ministry. We are not our own, for Jesus paid such a high price with His precious Blood for us. *"Or do you not know that your body is the temple of the Holy Spirit who is in you, whom you have from God, and you are not your own? For you were bought at a price; therefore glorify God in your body and in your spirit, which are God's" (1 Corinthians 6:19-20).*

How is that going to affect me now that God has my attention and has so graciously saved me from a horrible destruction as a lost and self-righteous person? Well, it is not just to go around finding all of the spiritual blessings and outpourings for my family, "me, my four and no more," all over the world. Instead, it will make me more aware of the need to absorb the Scripture daily and let the supernatural powerful Word of God permeate my heart. *"So shall My Word be that goes forth from My mouth; It shall not return to Me void, but it shall accomplish what I please, and it shall prosper in the thing for which I sent it" (Isaiah 55:11).*

Will the Word of God supernaturally change my circumstances? Yes, but we are made to be more than merely blessed people of God who chase around searching to be more "doubly-bubbly blessed" than we were yesterday. We are created in His image for His glory. We are created to be a blessing. We must be willing to take up our cross daily, no matter how heavy or hard to bear. Sometimes this is not so easy and can be nearly intolerable, but this is obedience to God through faith. *"...and come, take up the cross, and follow Me" (Mark 10:21b).* Whenever the load seems too hard or heavy to carry by ourselves, we need to turn to a trusted pastor or friend for prayer and encouragement. We have to remember that even Jesus for a few moments had some help carrying His cross by a person nearby.

It will all be worthwhile when by our obedience to God in carrying our cross daily, He is given much deserved glory. Since this life is just a fleeting moment in forever, we must look with an eternal perspective, keeping our eyes focused on our Savior. *"While we do not look at the things which are seen, but at the things which are not seen. For the things which are seen are temporary, but the things which are not seen are eternal" (2 Corinthians 4:18).* The Lord is the author and the finisher of our faith and when we look on things that are eternal, we keep our focus on finishing the race and achieving the goal or prize. *"I press toward the goal for the prize of*

the upward call of God in Christ Jesus"
(Philippians 3:14).

When compared to eternity, our extremely difficult circumstances seem much more bearable and astoundingly temporary. The joy of our salvation will be such a blessing, and we will stay full of peace in knowing and loving Jesus our Lord and Savior. Just the absolute understanding that we have salvation through Jesus Christ will be enough to see us through the most difficult times of our lives. Then we will even be there for many others, to share and help those with the heavy loads of their crosses to bear.

"Dear friends, don't be surprised at the fiery trials you are going through, as if something strange were happening to you. Instead, be very glad—because these trials will make you partners with Christ in His suffering, and afterward you will have the wonderful joy of

sharing His glory when it is displayed to all the world. *Be happy if you are insulted for being a Christian, for then the glorious Spirit of God will come upon you. If you suffer, however, it must not be for murder, stealing, making trouble, or prying into other people's affairs. But it is no shame to suffer for being a Christian.*

"Praise God for the privilege of being called by His wonderful name! For the time has come for judgment, and it must begin first among God's own children. And if even we Christians must be judged, what terrible fate awaits those who have never believed God's Good News? And if the righteous are barely saved, what chance will the godless and sinners have? So if you are suffering according to God's will, keep on doing what is right, and trust yourself to the God who

made you, for He will never fail you" (1 Peter
4:12-19 NLT).

"And now abide faith, hope, love, these three; but the greatest of these is love." 1 Corinthians 13:13

"For God so loved the world that He gave His only begotten Son, that whoever believes in Him should not perish but have everlasting life." John 3:16

"And now abide faith, hope, love, these three;
but the greatest of these is love." 1 Corinthians 13:13

"For God so loved the world that He gave His only
begotten Son, that whoever believes in Him should
not perish but have everlasting life." John 3:16

Chapter 15

Love is Serving!

I once had a crisis-related "pity party," and a minister friend told me that one of the best therapies during a crisis is to just go out and find someone that needs help or a ministry that needs extra people to serve. He gently mentioned to me that doing so often helps ease the pain from the tests and trials we go through. It works for me! Serving people even when it is difficult is a true demonstration of God's unconditional love. This willingness to give others our time, efforts and kindness is a supernatural miracle made possible by the presence of the Holy Spirit. Although it is a miracle, we actually have to make this decision to get up and do what is needed. It also helps us forget our self-focused issues, as we serve those who are much less fortunate than we are.

My mother-in-law, Dorothy Montgomery, is a very wise woman who has always exemplified this kind of serving love. She once told me a saying that she asked her five children many times as they were growing up. "How do you spell Love?" she would question. Then she would wait patiently for an answer that normally came out, "L—O—V—E." Afterward she would respond, "No, the correct answer is …H—E—L—P!" She also said, "Do not just tell me you love me, but show it by your actions of serving and helping."

I could not agree more! I really look forward to her frequent extended visits since Hurricane Katrina destroyed her neighborhood in Biloxi, Mississippi. This gives me the perfect opportunity to love and help. As an added benefit, the law of sowing and reaping applies here also. We end up helping ourselves by helping others. It is an excellent way to put "feet on our prayers," or faith in action, to bring about God's will.

"What does it profit, my brethren, if someone says he has faith but does not have works? Can faith save him? If a brother or sister is naked and destitute of daily food, and one of you says to them, 'Depart in peace, be warmed and filled,' but you do not give them the things which are needed for the body, what does it profit? Thus also faith by itself, if it does not have works, is dead. But someone will say, 'You

have faith, and I have works.' Show me your faith without your works, and I will show you my faith by my works.

"You believe that there is one God. You do well. Even the demons believe—and tremble! But do you want to know, O foolish man, that faith without works is dead? Was not Abraham our father justified by works when he offered Isaac his son on the altar? Do you see that faith was working together with his works, and by works faith was made perfect? And the Scripture was fulfilled which says, 'Abraham believed God, and it was accounted to him for righteousness.' And he was called the friend of God. You see then that a man is justified by works, and not by faith only" (James 2:14-24).

"And now abide faith, hope, love, these three; but the greatest of these is love." 1 Corinthians 13:13

"For God so loved the world that He gave His only begotten Son, that whoever believes in Him should not perish but have everlasting life." John 3:16

"And now abide faith, hope, love, these three; but the greatest of these is love." 1 Corinthians 13:13

"For God so loved the world that He gave His only begotten Son, that whoever believes in Him should not perish but have everlasting life." John 3:16

Chapter 16

Transformed Leaders— Developed by God

Near the beginning of this book there is an example of the selfless and caring people that we all desired to be around. These people thought of others more than themselves. They graciously listened to our every word; they could not get enough of our conversation and really cared. Well, all these selfless types of people are not born that way. God transforms the true servants of the Lord from the inside out. It begins with a "spiritual heart transplant." Our spiritual lives were not designed to hinge on a couple of weekly church services or sermons by a preacher. Our growth comes from our daily walk and talk with God and accountability with a small group family, whether inside a church building or in someone's home.

You are very special, unique and wonderfully created by God for a specific purpose. *"For You formed my inward parts; You covered me in my mother's womb. I will praise You, for I am fearfully and wonderfully made; marvelous are Your works, and that my soul knows very well. My frame was not hidden from You, when I was made in secret, and skillfully wrought in the lowest parts of the earth, Your eyes saw my substance, being yet unformed. And in Your*

book they all were written, the days fashioned for me, when as yet there were none of them" **(Psalms 139:13-16).**

Fulfillment of God's purpose for your life is only obtained through accepting Jesus Christ as your Lord and Savior and then deciding to allow Him to be the Ruler of all the kingdoms of your heart. Jesus said it about Himself as He was about to be crucified, ***"Most assuredly, I say to you, unless a grain of wheat falls into the ground and dies, it remains alone; but if it dies, it produces much grain. He who loves his life will lose it, and he who hates his life in this world will keep it for eternal life"*** **(John 12:24-25).**

It is always a matter of "dying to self" in order to truly live. Find your ministry in a small intimate group that will be your daily family of love, a genuine, agape love.

When we were in the flesh, we were trying to get on the cross and do everything ourselves. In contrast, Christ taught us by example and told us that He did nothing apart from His Father. When we deny self, we realize that we are not able to do it alone. We acknowledge our dependence on Jesus in order to give us strength to live this life totally committed to God. We did so when we received Jesus Christ as our Lord. We will probably never find our ministry fulfillment by only attending a church service once in awhile in a large group gathering, and Jesus never intended for that to be our spiritual model either. We need to pick a night or set a consistent time during the day to get our family and friends in a circle of fellowship, love, prayer and worship. It is enjoyable and brings unity.

Real abundant life is only obtained when we die to our self-will just as Jesus died doing the will of

God. We must lay our lives down at the cross and by faith accept that He is the Son of God. If He is our Lord, then we know He will do what He says He will do. We then accept that we cannot serve two masters. We then lay that old flesh man down, and he is buried. We must arise from our dead self and live in Jesus Christ, our Savior. *"...being confident of this, that He who began a good work in you will carry it on to completion until the day of Christ Jesus" (Philippians 1:6 NIV).*

Then from our obedience and His amazing grace comes the resurrected new person that can only come forth through the transformation of our spirit by the Blood of Jesus Christ. He paid the ultimate price. Jesus Christ paid it once and for all. He will never have to die on a cross and suffer all the shame, humility and weight of sin on His body again. He fulfilled this one lonely day when Almighty God could not look upon sin, and Jesus Christ obediently died for you and me. That is incomprehensible grace! This unmerited favor and *God's Greatest Gift of Love* was given because God loved us more than we could ever understand or imagine. ***"For God so loved the world that He gave His only begotten Son, that whoever believes in Him should not perish but have everlasting life" (John 3:16).***

Almighty God planned this redemption for us, bringing us out of our inherited fallen state and placing us in position to be restored to rightful fellowship with our Creator. It is absolutely miraculous grace. It is the type of grace not designed to be humanly possible; it is only supernaturally possible. Jesus has broken the yoke of sin, making it possible to connect the spiritual and physical realms. Miracles occur daily because of His sacrifice and the power in the name of Jesus—Yeshua the Messiah.

In light of such love from Jesus Christ our Savior, we will want to adopt His serving lifestyle and example of unconditional love. Jesus Christ paid it all by His obedient display of marvelous love to die a criminal's death of shame on a common cross. Will God allow man, created in His image, to become his own king and thus reject the plan God designed before the foundations of the earth? God said that it would be like trampling the sacrificed Blood of His Son under our feet. As the Word of God clearly says in Hebrews 10:29 NASB, *"How much severer punishment do you think he will deserve who has trampled under foot the Son of God, and has regarded as unclean the blood of the covenant by which he was sanctified, and has insulted the Spirit of grace?"*

The first assurance of our salvation is that our desires have changed entirely, and we are able to honestly say for the first time, "I will not play games with God ever again." Once we have the knowledge and presence of the saving grace of the Blood of Jesus genuinely in our lives, then we can have the assurance of our salvation.

We do not have to be ashamed of the Gospel, and we will find ourselves wanting to tell others about our new life of freedom in Jesus. We have a whole new set of standards. We are not better than anyone else; we are just transformed by God's "saving grace" from being eternally lost. Oh, what a difference! Now we find ourselves wanting to serve our fellow believers and others in need. We now want to belong not only to the "peripheral Sunday pew group" but we also want to belong to an intimate spiritual family group who ministers to the lost and to one another.

Now we can see how the one who hung on our every word as a good listener did so. We begin to understand the role of unconditional love for the world around us that is caught up in the devil's games. We now genuinely care for others.

"We love Him because He first loved us" *(1 John 4:19).*

"Love suffers long and is kind; love does not envy; love does not parade itself, is not puffed up; does not behave rudely, does not seek its own, is not provoked, thinks no evil; does not rejoice in iniquity, but rejoices in truth; bears all things, believes all things, hopes all things, endures all things. Love never fails..." *(1 Corinthians 13: 4-8a).*

"And now abide faith, hope, love, these three; but the greatest of these is love." 1 Corinthians 13:13

"For God so loved the world that He gave His only begotten Son, that whoever believes in Him should not perish but have everlasting life." John 3:16

Chapter 17

Love Never Fails

Remember that love never fails and endures all things. Love never ends. Everything hinges on our lifestyle of unconditional love. This is the kind of love that can only come from our Father through His Son Jesus Christ.

It is humanly and fleshly impossible to love the unlovable. Yet, with the supernatural power of the Holy Spirit, we can return good for evil, serve our fellow man and live lifestyles that deny self to follow Jesus.

"But I say to you who hear: Love your enemies, do good to those who hate you, bless those who curse you, and pray for those who spitefully use you. To him who strikes you on the one cheek, offer the other also. And from him who takes away your cloak, do not withhold your tunic either. Give to everyone who asks of you. And from him who takes away your goods do not ask them back. And just as you want men to do to you, you also do to them likewise. But if you love those who love you, what credit is that to you? For even sinners love those who love them. And if you do good to those who do good to you, what credit is that to you? For even sinners do the same. And if you lend to those from whom you hope to receive back, what credit is that to you? For even sinners lend to sinners to receive as much back. But love your

enemies, do good, and lend, hoping for nothing in return; and your reward will be great, and you will be sons of the Most High. For He is kind to the unthankful and evil. Therefore be merciful, just as your Father also is merciful" *(Luke 6:27-36).*

This is the amazing kind of love that causes a person to leave family, homelands, comforts or personal gain to go and help save the lost in foreign countries who worship other gods.

And He said to them, "Go into all the world and preach the Gospel to every creature" (Mark 16:15).

"And now abide faith, hope, love, these three; but the greatest of these is love." 1 Corinthians 13:13

"For God so loved the world that He gave His only begotten Son, that whoever believes in Him should not perish but have everlasting life." John 3:16

Chapter 18

Love God First

Jesus said it best in Matthew 22:37-40, *"'You shall love the Lord your God with all your heart, with all your soul, and with all your mind.' This is the first and great commandment. And the second is like it: 'You shall love your neighbor as yourself.' On these two commandments hang all the Law and the Prophets."*

Let unconditional love be our reflection. So as others look at us they literally see the Love of our Lord Jesus. They are seeing Jesus because they see His Love reflected in us. Then they cannot help but love the Jesus in us.

Let us read the entire chapter of 1st Corinthians 13 as we make this kind of Love our renewed heartfelt declaration to the Lord. Let us pray this scripture to the Lord from our heart.

"Though I speak with the tongues of men and of angels, but have not love, I have become sounding brass or a clanging cymbal. And though I have the gift of prophecy, and understand all mysteries and all knowledge, and though I have all faith, so that I could remove mountains, but have not love, I am nothing.

"And though I bestow all my goods to feed the poor, and though I give my body to be burned, but have not love, it profits me nothing. Love suffers long and is kind; love does not envy; love does not parade itself, is not puffed up; does not behave rudely, does not seek its own, is not provoked, thinks no evil; does not rejoice in iniquity, but rejoices in the truth; bears all things, believes all things, hopes all things, endures all things.

"Love never fails. But whether there are prophecies, they will fail; whether there are tongues, they will cease; whether there is knowledge it will vanish away. For we know in part and we prophesy in part. But when that which is perfect has come, then that which is in part will be done away.

"When I was a child, I spoke as a child, I understood as a child, I thought as a child; but when I became a man, I put away childish things. For now we see in a mirror, dimly, but then face to face. Now I know in part, but then I shall know just as I also am known. And now abide faith, hope, love, these three; but the greatest of these is love."

Love is the genuine gift of God for His creation through the death, burial and resurrection of His only begotten Son, Jesus Christ. It was God's love for a creation lost by the sin of the first Adam that caused Him to send us our Savior, the last Adam. Jesus Christ paid the price for us to travel back up the road that led from the Garden of Eden to the Cross of Calvary. Now we can love the Lord with all our heart, our soul and our mind. As we do this, others will definitely notice our unconditional love given daily, a sacrificial gift of service only a "born-again Christian" can possess. We take that lifestyle of love and model it to fellow Christians through the first example of the church that Christ gave us—in our new intimate spiritual family. Then, as we bring in the lost, we have a real loving spiritual family that will surround them. Whenever we meet together, we can present this fruit of unconditional love to all those hungry for more of Jesus' presence. This precious fruit will be fruit that remains because they are loved unconditionally. It takes unconditional love to win for Jesus a person who was born into a sinful world system.

"I say to you that likewise there will be more joy in heaven over one sinner who repents than over ninety-nine just persons who need no repentance" (Luke 15:7).

Just like you and me, they were destined for destruction at one time because of the fallen angel, satan. Once and for all time Jesus Christ won the battle over the forces of the enemy and now has the keys of hell and death.

"I am He who lives, and was dead, and behold, I am alive forevermore. Amen. And I have the keys of Hades and of Death" (Revelation 1:18).

We do not have to fight the battle any longer. God said, *"It is finished!"* Now simply love the unlovable by obeying the Father and displaying what He has so freely given us. We need to give back to those who are now just as we were before Jesus drew us unto Him. Now we will become like the people in the previous example who cared enough to put their arm around us in our former lost condition. Jesus paid the price and all we have to do is realize it and live through Him for His sake. We learn by example, we live by example and now hopefully we give by example.

So, how do I get it? Give the love of Jesus away. Just share the Gospel and that blessing of your never-ending life in Jesus Christ with someone today. Let unconditional love be spoken as loud in your life as it is in your words. We will then be found always in Love with God.

Then we can truly thank God for His Greatest Gift—Love!

"For I am persuaded that neither death nor life, nor angels nor principalities nor powers, nor things present nor things to come, nor height nor depth, nor any other created thing, shall be able to separate us from the love of God which is in Christ Jesus our Lord" (Romans 8:38-39).

"Dear friends, let us love one another, for love comes from God. Everyone who loves has been born of God and knows God. Whoever does not love does not know God, because God is love. This is how God showed His love among us: He sent His one and only Son into the world that we might live through Him. This is love: not that we loved God, but that He loved us and sent His Son as an atoning sacrifice for our sins" (1 John 4:7-10 NIV).

"Love the LORD your God with all your heart and with all your soul and with all your strength" (Deuteronomy 6:5NIV).

REFLECTIONS

REFLECTIONS

REFLECTIONS

REFLECTIONS

REFLECTIONS

REFLECTIONS

REFLECTIONS

To obtain additional copies of this book, other information and/or materials
contact:

Word to the World Ministries
Baker, LA   70704-0879
225.771.1774

www.wordtotheworldministries.org

LOVE God's Greatest Gift
CD AUDIO BOOK
READ BY THE AUTHOR
John Mark Pool
Order your copy today for $17.00

Word to the World Ministries
P.O. Box 879
Baker, LA   70704-0879
225.771.1774
www.wordtotheworldministries.org

John Mark Pool, guest with Sid Roth's "It's Supernatural" TV Show

Word to the World Ministries
wholeheartedly recommends
to view and support

You may go online and enjoy the radio or
TV program *"It's Supernatural"*
Watch John Mark Pool's TV interview
Archives Date Aug. 8-15, 2005
www.SidRoth.org
Messianic Vision
P.O. Box 1918 • Brunswick, GA 31521

Phone: (912) 265-2500
Fax: (912) 265-3735
Orders: (800) 548-1918
Customer Service Phone: (912) 265-2500, Ext. 17

DVD AVAILABLE of the JOHN MARK POOL TV INTERVIEW
Contact Word to the World Ministries   225.771.1774

P.O. Box 879 • Baker, LA 70704
www.wordtotheworldministries.org

Another book scheduled for release May 1, 2007

by John Mark Pool

Path of the Prophet

Understanding the Journey

John Mark Pool reveals his life's journey from a young boy to the present, detailing his spiritual, ministry and marital experiences. His childhood was spent in an idyllic rural 1950's environment, where his family, especially his mother, played an important role in building his spiritual foundation. His teenage, college and subsequent years were spent in the city. He became involved in many worldly vices that ultimately entailed winning and losing fortunes and more. Though throughout his life he has faced abandonment, death, banishment and betrayal, he clings nonetheless to his love of the Lord Jesus to see him through each situation.

Path of the Prophet

Paperback $15.99
ISBN 978-0-7684-2442-3

Available wherever Christian books are sold,
or contact: Destiny Image® Publishers, Inc.

Toll Free 1.800.722.6774
P.O. Box 310 • Shippensburg, PA 17257-0310
www.destinyimage.com

www.wordtotheworldministries.org

Word to the World Ministries
Prophetic Training School ©

PROPHETIC FOUNDATION LEVELS I & II

ADVANCED LEVELS III & IV

Evangelizing † Training † Activating † Releasing

www.wordtotheworldministries.org
P.O. Box 879 • Baker, LA 70704
225.771.1774

Contact Word to the World Ministries to: Schedule
Prophetic Training School - Basic Training Levels I & II
and/or Advanced Prophetic Training Levels III & IV for your
region or obtain information on upcoming scheduled courses

John Mark Pool & Steve Shultz, founder/host
Ministering on a Prophetic TV Program

Word to the World Ministries
highly recommends:

Elijah Rain Prophetic Magazine
&
www.Prophetic.tv

The Elijah List
www.elijahlist.com

Phone: 866.354.5354

310 2nd Ave. SE ▪ Albany, OR 97321

John Mark Pool teaching on WGCB TV program Channel 49 Red Lion, PA

John Mark Pool teaches Prophetic Training Schools I II III & IV in many locations each year across the USA and around the world

John Mark Pool teaching in a barn called the Ark of Safety Vincennes, IN

John Mark Pool's fiery & anointed preaching at a fellowship meeting in a shopping center

A True Love Story from Heaven©
Future Release Scheduled for 2008

John Mark is currently writing the new book entitled
A True Love Story from Heaven.

Our Love Story promises to be like a "fairy tale romance novel," yet it is filled with miracles that prove you can find true love!

Thank you for all you have done and especially for your prayers and continued support. We bless you now in the precious name of Jesus!
All our Love in Him,

John Mark & Sandy Pool

204